Other books produced by Colin and Eithne

The *Picturing Scotland* Series: a book for every part of Scotland

Aberdeen
Aberdeenshire
Argyll
The Isle of Arran
Arran & Ayrshire
The Borders
The Cairngorms
Caithness & Sutherland
Caledonia
Coll & Tiree
Distinguished Distilleries*
Dumfries & Galloway
Dundee
Dundee & Angus
Edinburgh
Fife, Kinross & Clackmannan
Glasgow
Inverness
Islay, Jura, Colonsay & Oronsay
Lanarkshire

Lochaber
Loch Lomond, Cowal & Bute
Loch Ness
The Lothians
Moray-Speyside
Mull & Iona
Orkney
Orkney in Wartime
The Outer Hebrides
The City of Perth*
Highland Perthshire*
Ross & Cromarty
Royal Deeside
Sacred Scotland
Scotland's Mountains
Scotland's Wildlife
Shetland
The Isle of Skye
Stirling & The Trossachs
The West Highland Way

Commissioned Books (*In-Camera* format)

The Cairngorm Reindeer Herd

On a Rising Tide by Charlie Phillips
A photographic celebration of Britain's largest Bottlenose dolphins
Large format: 10" x 10"

ABERFELDY & KENMORE

AN *IN-CAMERA* BOOK

Colin Nutt
Author and photographer

NESS PUBLISHING

2 Loch Tay viewed from Kenmore beach. At 24kms/15 miles long, it's the largest loch in Perthshire. With a maximum depth of 155m/508ft it is also one of the deepest in Scotland. To the north, the loch is

ABERFELDY & KENMORE

flanked by the impressive bulk of the Ben Lawers mountain range. In addition to Ben Lawers itself, this comprises a further seven Munros (Scottish mountains higher than 914m/3000ft).

Welcome to Aberfeldy & Kenmore!

The charming town of Aberfeldy and the delightful village of Kenmore nestle in Strathtay, Strathtay lies right at the heart of Perthshire and Perthshire lies right at the heart of Scotland. This is where Perthshire's highest mountain (Ben Lawers) and the source of Scotland's longest and most volatile river (the Tay) are to be found.

Aberfeldy is thought to go back to 1796, as building leases were granted that year. Industries such as cotton milling, dating from 1799, figured among the town's beginnings, as did distilling (inevitably!). Today, Dewar's Aberfeldy Distillery is the town's principal tourist attraction. Choosing to establish a settlement here was probably due to the fact that the location was already a bridging point, thanks to General Wade's construction in 1733 of the fine bridge that still stands today (see p.10 and back cover). It was part of his 10-year campaign of building roads and bridges across the Highlands to facilitate the movement of troops. Standing by the bridge is another of Aberfeldy's notable landmarks, the memorial to the Black Watch Highland Regiment, which first assembled here in 1740. The name 'Black Watch' comes from the dark tartans the soldiers wore. The monument cost about £500, raised by public subscription – a process rather like today's 'crowdfunding'.

The area that became Aberfeldy got its first recognition from 1787 following Robert Burns' visit that year and his song, *The Birks of Aberfeldy*, which shows the name already represented the area. Like so many places, Aberfeldy got a great boost from the arrival of the railway in 1865 which led to the town

Aberfeldy in its Strathtay setting. The town's name comes from the Gaelic *Abair Pheallaig*, meaning the mouth of Pheallaig Burn.

becoming something of an inland resort. This goes some way to explaining the large number of fine Victorian and Edwardian villas in the town today, particularly towards the river. The usual leisure pursuits followed – golf course, bowls club, tennis courts – which have left their architectural mark in the form of clubhouses and pavilions. The town's first council convened in 1887.

A short journey of six miles west along the A827 leads to Kenmore, a most picturesque village thanks to the charming and cohesive appearance that derives from its planned-village redevelopment by the Earl of Breadalbane from 1755. It was built approximately on the site of the earlier settlement thought to have been known as Inchadnie. Kenmore's position at the outlet (east) end of Loch Tay gives it first-class views down the loch – and towards the Scottish Crannog Centre, a short distance from Kenmore where the 21st Century Crannog Community provides a fascinating journey into Scotland's prehistory. Visitors can walk in

The impressive obelisks of Aberfeldy's Tay Bridge, added to the bridge in 1734, the year after it was built.

the footsteps of the original Crannog dwellers, be immersed in village life with original artefacts, demonstrations of textiles, cooking and ancient crafts and technologies or take a replica log-boat for a paddle in the loch around the atmospheric Crannog Roundhouse.

Strathtay is a beautiful little slice of Scotland. Those who come here love to return for another dose of clear air, open space and endless views of the surrounding mountains – all within a distance of 12 miles or so from east to west. With a number of excellent hotels in both Kenmore and Aberfeldy, each with its own blend of comfort, cuisine and warm hospitality, staying here offers all manner of outdoor pursuits, whether vigorous or leisurely, in an area of outstanding natural beauty. This book was written to provide an insight into this majestic land and will be an aid to those who plan to visit for the first time and a lasting reminder and a 'haste ye back' to those who have already experienced its loveliness.

Seen from the Tay Bridge, the Black Watch Memorial catches the first light of an autumn day.

8   From an elevated position on the south side of Strathtay near Aberfeldy, an autumn view that captures the essence of this part of Perthshire. It's only late October, but the first snows have already fallen on

the tops. Most of the autumn colour is on the larch trees – the only conifers which are not evergreens.

10 On the northern edge of Aberfeldy, the Tay Bridge (also known as General Wade's Bridge) opened in October 1733. It is almost 122m/400ft in overall length with the centre arch measuring 18m/60ft.

Left: close-up of the statue atop the Black Watch Memorial which stands by the river in Aberfeldy. Erected in 1887, it commemorates the first mustering of the regiment in 1740. Right: salmon sculpture.

12 Aberfeldy has many fine examples of Victorian and Edwardian villas. This one is opposite the well-tended gardens by Taybridge Road. Spot the bicycle sculpture!

Just around the corner on Taybridge Terrace is Aberfeldy Golf Club, the clubhouse of which is pictured here. Founded in 1895, it is a very scenic 9-hole course. Just visible towards the right . . .

14 Left . . . is the elegant modern suspension footbridge across the Tay. Right: Aberfeldy Parish Church is a congregation within the Church of Scotland, active in many aspects of Christian life and service.

The Aberfeldy Watermill Bookshop, Gallery and Café is a three-storey former oatmeal mill in the centre of Aberfeldy. It was opened in 2005 by Michael Palin.

16 The town retains other traditional shops such as Doigs of Aberfeldy on Bank Street, pictured here. An outfitter to ladies and gentlemen, with all its other departments, it's a veritable Aladdin's Cave!

Left: in the north-west corner of The Square is the Locus Centre, which houses the Tourist Information Centre among other things. Right: the beautifully preserved 1885 drinking fountain.

18 The Birks Cinema in Aberfeldy opened in 1939. Following closure in the 1980s, this fine Art Deco building has been superbly restored, re-opening in 2013. It now provides the town with a state-of-the-art rural

cinema, complete with a welcoming Café-Bar open daily from mid-morning 'til late all year round. It also hosts special screenings and events.

20 Near the entrance to the new Reflection Garden (opened 2018) in the Lower Birks, is one of two specially made iron benches with images of soldiers, doves and poppies welded into the design.

Aberfeldy has much to offer, high on the list being the famous Birks (birches). The Moness Burn tumbles down the ravine through the Birks towards the town. Especially colourful in autumn . . .

22 . . . when scenes like this abound. Originally known as the Den of Moness, the area was renamed after a song written by Robert Burns following his visit in August 1787.

At the top of the Birks gorge, the burn plunges down the Upper Moness Falls which are at their most spectacular in full spate as in this winter view from above.

24 In the coldest of winters, the falls can freeze up completely, giving rise to extraordinary scenes like these – sheer joy for ice-climbing enthusiasts.

Almost as extraordinary in its very different way, this lichen-covered tree in the Birks has been brought down by flood or landslide and now rests horizontally above the burn.

26 Aberfeldy's many characterful buildings include the 1906-built Old Pavilion with its Arts & Crafts touches. Located at Aberfeldy Bowling Club, it also serves the tennis courts behind.

A benefit of Aberfeldy's relatively remote location is that views of the surrounding countryside can be enjoyed from the town, such as this west-facing shot with everything from harvest bales to Ben Lawers.

28 Dewar's Aberfeldy Distillery is one of the town's main attractions, offering tours and tastings for its many visitors. In 1898, the stills first produced the beautifully balanced single malt whisky which is

at the heart of the Dewar's blend. Whisky tours at the distillery take place throughout the day and include access to its excellent heritage exhibition.

30 Until the 1960s, a branch railway line reached Aberfeldy, allowing the whisky to be transported by train. The distillery retains its shunting locomotive and a loaded wagon for visitors to see.

This long-range shot from just outside Aberfeldy looks north-west across the intervening slopes to Schiehallion (1083m/3553ft), arguably Perthshire's most prominent mountain, although not the highest.

32   A couple of miles east of Aberfeldy at Grandtully, St Mary's Church retains this magnificent painted ceiling that dates back to the 1600s. A very rare survivor and truly a sight to behold!

Taken from St Mary's, this picture captures how wintry conditions bring out different aspects of the countryside that have their own appeal, even if it's a dreich day like this one.

34   The River Tay at Grandtully is the main base for canoe and kayak slalom and racing in Scotland. Here, a youngster learns how to manage the rapids.

Now moving a couple of miles west of Aberfeldy, Bolfracks House has a long history. A map in the house shows it was there in 1769, although the Gothic front seen above was added c.1838.

36 The house is best known for its gardens. There has been an ornamental garden here since the mid-18th century, but most of what can be seen today is the effort of the late Mr J. Douglas Hutchinson

since 1975. As well as the wonderful gardens themselves, the hillside location gives excellent long views along the strath, in this case to the east and including the distant Castle Menzies . . .

38 . . . which, with the help of a long lens, is seen more clearly in its sylvan setting. The castle's walled garden can also be made out, to its right. More of Castle Menzies later (see pages 74-75).

A further two miles or so west, adjacent to the A827, is Croft Moraig Stone Circle. It is rated as the most spectacular of all Perthshire's many stone circles and is certainly the most complex.

40   Croft Moraig comprises a series of three concentric circles begun about 3000BC. The first was made of wooden posts, later replaced by a circle of eight stones. Some time after that, an outer circle of nine

large stones was added. These range from 1.75 – 2.1 metres tall. Most of the stones are still standing. Various astronomical alignments have been identified at the site.

42 Another benefit of stopping at Croft Moraig is the sight of Schiehallion looming up to the north, now much closer than when first seen on p.31.

Another mile west brings the first sighting of Loch Tay. The mist of a dull January day adds a frisson of mystery. The wetter conditions of these times encourage lichen to flourish on the trees.

44 And so to the lovely village of Kenmore, with its idyllic setting at the end of Loch Tay. Kenmore was rebuilt by the Earl of Breadalbane as a planned estate village from 1755.

The heart of Kenmore is The Square, a broad street lined with cosy-looking white cottages and, as seen here, the village Post Office and shop. Walking to the end of this row leads to . . .

46 ... Kenmore Parish Church, built 1760. More accurately, it was a reconstruction of the earlier building which added the transepts and the tower. The churchyard and church green were also laid out then.

The interior of Kenmore Church. The south transept window's theme is Praise to the Creator and the two main figures (in the centre panels) are King David and John the Baptist.

48 Another historic building in Kenmore is its fine hotel, said to be Scotland's oldest inn, built as a tavern in 1502. In 1572 Laird Colin Campbell commissioned the structure and created the hotel.

An aerial view of Mains of Taymouth Country Estate in Kenmore, which provides luxury accommodation, a golf course, restaurant and riding stables. It is also an excellent venue for weddings and other events.

50   The eastern end of The Square is dominated by the imposing gateway which forms the western entrance to the Taymouth Castle Estate, encompassing 450 acres, at the heart of which is

Taymouth Castle. This vast and imposing edifice was built from 1802 to 1842. In 2004 its conversion to a luxury hotel began and which, after various interruptions, continues to this day.

52 At the time of writing, another new would-be owner is attempting to purchase the castle.
Left: the central section of the castle. Right: the opulent interior of one of its restored salons.

Returning to Kenmore, this is the beach at the end of Loch Tay. On the left is one of the attractive floral displays crowned by a salmon sculpture, like those found in Aberfeldy.

54 The beach itself is a wonderful vantage point for views down the loch, especially when including the tree-covered islet (once a crannog) on the left. The snow-capped summit of Ben Lawers

draws the eye and warrants closer inspection, on this day when snow cover extended further down its slopes. It is Scotland's 10th-highest mountain at 1214m/3983ft, but it's not a hard climb.

56 We bid farewell to Kenmore by admiring it from the Black Rock viewpoint on Drummond Hill. Kenmore Bridge, built 1774, actually has seven arches, but the smaller ones at each end are hidden from view.

The bridge marks the start of the River Tay, from where it begins its 120-mile journey to the North Sea, making it Scotland's longest river.

58 As noted on p.55, thanks to a high start point, the ascent of Ben Lawers is not too demanding. The route crosses the summit of Beinn Ghlas (1103m/3619ft), seen here from the top of Ben Lawers.

Turning to look north from Ben Lawers' summit reveals the craggy pair of An Stuc (it simply means 'the peak') and Meall Garbh ('Rough Hill'), which share the same height of 1118m/3668ft.

60 An unusual view of the Scottish Crannog Centre, located on the south shore of Loch Tay near Kenmore, but photographed here from Drummond Hill on the north side of the loch.

The Crannog during the Samhain festival on 31st October. Opened following the reconstruction of an Iron Age crannog as an archaeological experiment, the Scottish Crannog Centre . . .

... has evolved over the years to become a museum with a unique insight into life in the Iron Age. Above: the walkway to the Crannog lit up in celebration of Samhain. Crannogs are a type of

ancient loch dwelling found widely throughout Scotland and Ireland. They had many uses, including as dwellings to accommodate extended families. Above: the Crannog's interior.

64 The climax of the Samhain celebration is the burning of a wicker creature, on this occasion in the form of a Kelpie. The labels that are hanging on it carry the wishes and hopes of those attending.

Left: the burning of the kelpie is accompanied by the playing of an early form of bagpipe.
Right: events like Samhain attract a host of colourful characters, such as Jack Frost spotted here.

66 A mile or so beyond the Crannog Centre is the village of Acharn, from where a steep walk of 15-20 minutes reaches the Hermit's Cave (left), which forms a 'secret' approach to the Falls of Acharn.

The highest drop of these falls is over 20m/65ft (opposite, right). Above: returning through the cave and continuing further up the track, this is an enticing view of more of the falls.

68 Enthusiasts of ancient history can continue this walk for about another half-hour to climb up to Falls of Acharn Stone Circle, the most dramatically positioned example in Perthshire.

Four of its nine stones still stand. On a day of moody light and shade, these two neatly frame part of the Ben Lawers mountain range in the distance.

70 Heading back towards Aberfeldy via the B846, from near the village of Dull, Highland Safaris offers exhilarating 4x4 safaris around the surrounding hills. Inset: at the HS Red Deer Centre. They also

provide a unique cruise on Loch Tay exploring the history, heritage and folklore to be found around this great loch. The view from the boat also gives a different perspective on the surrounding landscape.

72 Having had a couple of sightings of Schiehallion, it's time for an idea of what the views from it are like. Access to Schiehallion is an approximately nine-mile drive north from Aberfeldy. The climb itself is

six miles and entails an ascent of 731m/2398ft. From about half-way up and looking roughly east, Loch Tummel makes a fine and extensive sight.

74 On the way back to Aberfeldy, Castle Menzies *has* to be visited. The Castle was the seat of Clan Menzies for over 500 years. Rescued as a ruin in 1957, it has been lovingly restored and is open to visitors.

Architecturally fascinating, it is a splendid Renaissance example of the transition in Scottish Castles from earlier rugged Highland fortresses to later mansion houses.

76 From Castle Menzies, it's only half-a-mile to the village of Weem – its hotel is pictured. The name Weem is derived from the Gaelic *uaimh*, meaning cave, where St Cuthbert is said to have lived.

The Old Kirk of Weem is thought to have been built in the mid 1400s and contains the Menzies Mausoleum. It has always been associated with St Cuthbert, who brought his ministry to Strathtay c.650.

78 Left: Dull & Weem Parish Church, in Weem, was built in 1875. Right upper: charming creatures in the churchyard! Right lower: inscription over the door of the Old Kirk of Weem (see p.77).

And so, having gone full circle from Aberfeldy to Kenmore and back again, here is a last look at the pastoral Perthshire landscape as seen from the east of Aberfeldy. A grand tour!

Published 2020 by Ness Publishing, 47 Academy Street, Elgin, Moray, IV30 1LR
Phone 01343 549663 www.nesspublishing.co.uk

All photographs © Colin and Eithne Nutt except p.24 (both) © Kevin Ramage;
p.29 © Dewar's Aberfeldy Distillery; pp.33, 44 & 54 © Alan Edwards;
p.49 © Mains of Taymouth Estate; pp.70 (both) & 71 © Highland Safaris

Printed in Malta

Text © Colin Nutt
ISBN 978-1-906549-86-2

All rights reserved. No part of this publication may be reproduced, stored in a retrieval system, in any form or by any means, without prior permission of Ness Publishing. The right of Colin Nutt as author of this work has been asserted by him in accordance with the Copyright, Designs and Patents Act 1988.

Front cover: the Black Watch Memorial in Aberfeldy; p.1: retired steam roller in Victoria Park, Aberfeldy; p.4: carved wooden statue of animals in Reflection Garden, Aberfeldy; this page: Reflection Garden, Aberfeldy; back cover: Tay/Wade's Bridge, Aberfeldy

While Ness Publishing takes care to ensure all information is accurate, no responsibility can be taken for errors, or changes that occur after the book has gone to press.

Picturing Scotland books which most relate to the area around Aberfeldy and Kenmore.

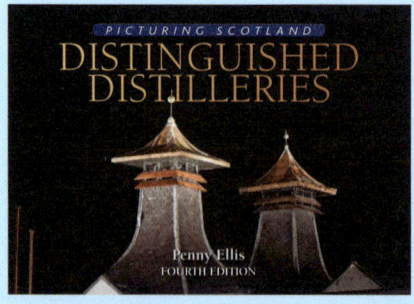

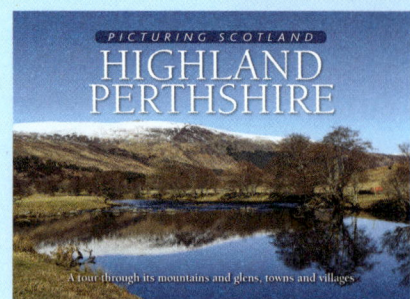

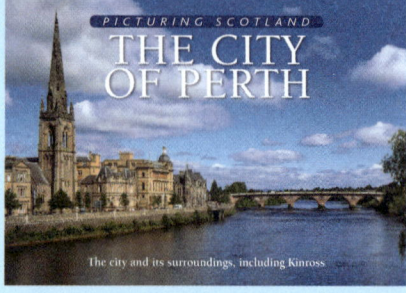